Your COMPLETE Guide to SUCCEEDING with LinkedIn:
The ULTIMATE Checklist of 85 STEPS
With Tips to Follow for
Establishing Your Presence, Being Noticed,
Getting Found, and Successfully HIRED!

Dr. Scott Dell

Copyright © 2020 Dr. Scott Dell

All rights reserved.

ISBN-13: 979-8-65-397364-2

Part of the **To MY Success Series**!

https://tinyurl.com/LinkedinSuccessGuide/

DEDICATION

We are not alone. In a demonstration of appreciation to those that came before me and directly influenced my efforts, as well as those that I currently serve as an educator and entrepreneur that still inspire me, I dedicate this book, paying it forward, to those that follow.

CONTENTS

	Acknowledgments	I
1	Introduction	1
2	What's a 1st Degree or 2nd Degree Connection?	3
3	The ABC's To Success	5
4	The Why & The Numbers	7
5	Getting Started at the Beginning	9
6	Getting Found – Boosting Your Profile	13
7	Enhancing Your Profile	16
8	Security and Privacy Considerations	23
9	Searches & Expanding Your Network	27
10	LinkedIn Strategies	42
11	Afterword	52
12	About the Author	53

ACKNOWLEDGMENTS

As a learner, I have been inspired by teachers, colleagues, peers, friends, and family. With too many to thank individually, I thank you all for your support and inspiration. As an academic and entrepreneur, I continue to be inspired by the same group above while adding a new group to learn from, my students and clients. What they may not realize is that as I endeavor to promote growth and learning, the reflection of those efforts come back and inspire me, helping me, and hopefully you, to grow and learn. Thank you all.
To Your Continued Success!

1 INTRODUCTION

LinkedIn, the final frontier. These are your voyages using LinkedIn to enhance your personal presence and professional career. Your lifetime mission, should you decide to accept it, is to explore LinkedIn's powerful and greatest features, to seek out new ways to improve your experience and results, to boldly take initiatives that improve your career opportunities while making society a better place for yourself and others!

If this sounds familiar, you might recognize this document's mission statement as inspired by two classic TV series, Star Trek and Mission Impossible. You do not have to wait until Stardate 2258.42 or be Mr. Phelps to succeed. YOU can start TODAY! What follows are specific actions with additional tips that will help you launch your personal, professional, and career success. Whether you are looking for a job, a customer, a vendor, a career, an internship, a colleague, a friend, or a date, applying the steps below will enhance your efforts so that you can succeed beyond, as in the Moody Blues song, "your wildest dreams."

This is your definitive guide to setting up and using your LinkedIn account that WILL get you established on this powerful platform. It is then up to you to reap the benefits.

Quick story about the experience of one of my students. In all my classes, starting about ten years ago, I require a LinkedIn assignment. Students need to set up an account, and if they already have one, they are given specific ways to enhance it. Mike (yes, that is his real name, but I won't give you his last) was a newer user of LinkedIn. He dutifully completed his assignment (and got an A on it) but approached me with a LinkedIn question about a month after completion. He said that he was contacted directly by someone he did not know from a company he didn't recognize. I actually got pretty excited for him when I heard the company name and recognized the person asking as one of my 1st degree connections. They were inquiring to see if he might be interested in an internship with their organization. He was asking about how to react. I used the inquiry as a teachable moment and had him research the company and the individual that contacted him using both LinkedIn and Google. What he had not realized is that this company, Northwestern Mutual Life (NML) was a Fortune 500 company with one of the best internship programs in the country! Not only did he interview, get hired, and succeed gloriously in the internship, he ended up in the top 5% of interns in the country. He now owns his own successful company in Wisconsin. All starting with a contact that he didn't know from a company that he had never heard of. LinkedIn DOES WORK!

2 WHAT'S A 1ST DEGREE OR 2ND DEGREE CONNECTION?

I want to discuss one terminology item that sometimes confuses people. What are 1st degree, 2nd degree, and 3rd degree connections and why is it important to understand these terms? With over 675 million users on LinkedIn, you have over 675M potential connections that you can reach out directly to and invite to become part of your network. When you send an invite and they accept, or you accept an invite from someone else, they become a 1st degree connection of yours. What that means is you can directly send them messages through InMail (like email, but internal to LinkedIn), and basically, have full access to their profile, if they include it, such as email, phone number, and other information. I find LinkedIn to be a convenient Rolodex making it easy to reach out to my 1st degree connections without having to track down email addresses or other ways to reach friends and colleagues.

A 2nd degree connection is a connection of someone else that you are not directly connected to THROUGH one of your 1st degree connections. Not being directly connected to you as a 1st degree connection means you cannot easily send them InMails or have access to other information. There is immense value in having a large network of 1st degree connections, especially when it comes to searches. When conducting a search, LinkedIn's search algorithm will first look at the 1st degree connections of the searcher, and then proceed to their second-degree connections, and then finally to 3rd degree connections, which are connections to your connections' connections (not confusing at all, right?), and then others in the LinkedIn user universe. As an example, if an HR manager is connected to me, and you are connected to me, that HR manager is now YOUR 2nd degree connection. If they do a search using keywords the search first flows through their 1st degree connections, me, AND THEN, proceeds to search their 2nd degree connections, which means they find YOU! With that understanding, let's go ahead and start tapping into the power of LinkedIn.

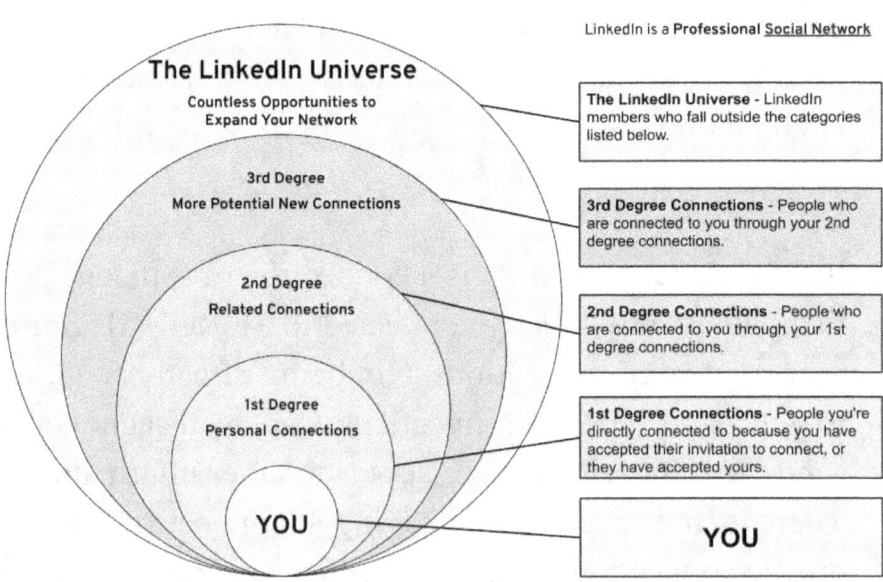

Connection Relationships Through the Eyes of LinkedIn

3 THE ABC'S TO SUCCESS

You know that a quality LinkedIn presence is crucial in creating a positive first impression as well as leaving a lasting impactful image, and being found for those seeking somebody with your skills and talents. The following step-by-step guide is structured to walk you through the setup to effectively use this incredibly powerful tool. Follow these ABCs and you WILL SUCCEED in making LinkedIn work for YOU!

Topics include:
- A. Basic Background as to THE WHY you want to use this powerful tool (Intro).
- B. LinkedIn by the Numbers (LinkedIn Statistics).
- C. Creating your account from scratch, THE HOW (1-18).
- D. Tips for BUILDING & BOOSTING YOUR PROFILE to firmly establish your online presence (19-23).
- E. Enhancing the depth of your profile to increase search-ability and getting found (24-36).
- F. Understanding and using the security and privacy setting available within LinkedIn (37-46).
- G. Conducting YOUR searches. Learn how to take advantage of the built-in power available for finding people and resources allowing you to build your network and enhance your effectiveness using this powerful tool. Streamline your process in

finding contacts, companies, groups, jobs, vendors, and customers (47-64).
H. Specific proactive ACTIONS TO TAKE that keep YOU top-of-mind and FOUND in searches (65-85).
I. Springboarding YOUR SUCCESS (Conclusion)!

This guide is designed to help new and existing users get the most from LinkedIn. As a step-by-step guide, even if you have never logged into LinkedIn before, you can start with step 1 and progress through the steps sequentially. This will help you to develop a stellar presence that WILL GET YOU RESULTS. If you already have a LinkedIn presence, I encourage you to read through Section C: creating your account, to make sure you are familiar with the terms and concepts associated. You might also want to double-check to make sure you didn't take too many shortcuts in establishing your presence. I would also encourage you to read this manual cover-to-cover BEFORE executing ANY of the steps, much like you would read the instruction booklet in full before assembling furniture so you don't put things on backwards. Then again, I never read those booklets in full either, so I would understand if you jump in starting with step 1 and move forward. I also encourage you to do one section at a time and NOT try to do it all in one sitting. To do the job right you want to make sure your submissions are well thought out with time to reflect. Good luck and enjoy.

4 THE WHY & THE NUMBERS

Background-The Why:

You have heard it before. You NEED to be on LinkedIn. But WHY? Everyone's why may be different. Are you looking for a job or new opportunity? Seeking new customers/clients? Wanting to find the best potential employees? Seeking to build a network or have a single source allowing easy access to your contacts - a modern Rolodex? Might you be researching people that you are meeting for the first time? Wanting a convenient place to keep up with job and education changes in your network, complete with reminders as they happen? Setting an example for coworkers, colleagues, family, or students? Promoting your own brand/image Keeping up with the Joneses? Do you want access to current company/industry/business news, updates and trends? Need a convenient place to store your work history, dates, and accomplishments for easy access? Want an accessible database for including your membership numbers in professional organizations or for your certifications (only visible to you)? Find old friends, alumni, former/current coworkers, or family members? Discovering reliable sources for making buying decisions? Performing research on schools or alumni to find where they live/work? Or do you think Microsoft was on to something when they paid over $26 Billion (with a B) for LinkedIn in 2016 – which comes out to about $60 per member? Maybe a combination of the above? YOU'RE IN THE RIGHT PLACE!

LinkedIn by The Numbers:
    A. Here are the facts and figures as of 2020:
LinkedIn was founded before Facebook in 2003.
Over 675M (million) current members with about half being considered active users.
On average, 2 members are added every second.
About ¼ of the members reside in the U.S - over 150M. With a U.S. population approximately 330M, that is quite a high percentage.
46M college students or recent grads are members globally with over 50% of U.S. college graduates using it.
57%/43% Male/Female split.
40ish% are premium members (plans start at $29 per month), but a free account can do SO much. Note: You can share opportunities, help others grow, post articles & videos, join groups, find employees, discover vendors, gain customers, and build your network to over 15,000 1st degree connections with a free account. I did.
Used by 92% of the Fortune 500.
Over 40% of the world's millionaires are members.
Used by over 95% of recruiters, over 97% of B2B marketers, and now YOU!

5 GETTING STARTED AT THE BEGINNING

Start from here to set up your account from scratch. If you are new to LinkedIn or have not yet set up your account, the steps in this section will get you started in creating your account. If you already have an account you could jump to section D., but I might encourage you to read through the following steps to reinforce some of the terms that will be used throughout this document.

Getting In. For those without an account do the following:
1. Go to the site: https://www.linkedin.com/.
2. Click *Join Now* in the Upper Right Corner.
3. Enter email and create a password in the next screen – click on *Agree & Join* (if you agree and want to join).
4. Enter First & Last Name – *Continue*.
5. Confirm you are NOT a robot.
6. Start creating your profile by answering questions – *Next*.
7. Enter your most recent job title, company, and industry if prompted OR click on I am a student. You can eventually do both but select the option here that is most pertinent or what you might want to be most recognized for. If you are starting a company, your new company would also be a good choice to begin with. Choose *continue*.

8. Confirm your email by entering the code sent to your account. *Agree & Confirm*.
9. Answer questions like "Are you looking for a new job" (Note: If you say yes, your intentions will stay confidential and only be accessible to recruiters).
10. Continue filling out profile information.
11. Optionally: Let LinkedIn send out emails to ALL of your email contacts. Personally, I would recommend against this. It is better to custom choose who you ultimately want in your network rather than send blanket invitations to your contacts. But, if you want to fast track growing your account you can let LinkedIn do the heavy lifting for you by reaching out to potential connections with this mass email feature. Choose *SKIP* if you rather not send mass emails at this time. You can still initiate this process at a later date.
12. Start searching for contacts that you want to add or choose from suggestions (Or skip for now). Click *Done* after entering each person and then click *Next* at the bottom to continue.
13. Add a PROFESSIONAL photo. There are options to use your Facebook or Google photo, but you will most likely want something else that projects professionalism. YOU NORMALLY GET MORE INVITES WITH A PICTURE. A professional headshot really does make a difference! This important step will be discussed further below.
14. Optionally connect with *teammates* followed by *Next* or *Skip*.

15. You may also create a job alert if you want LinkedIn to send you leads. Options for title and location may be entered here or choose *Skip*.
16. Load the LinkedIn app on your mobile device by entering your phone number and choosing *Text me the link* (recommended), or you can *Skip*.
17. Select companies and people from suggestions to "*follow*" if you would like to keep up on industry trends or insights from thought leaders.
18. Click *Finish* YOU'RE IN!

Your profile is the first place to focus if you want to enhance your effectiveness in using LinkedIn. LinkedIn search algorithms are designed to find you if you want to be found, but you must set yourself up for success by: 1. Having a professional photo; 2. FULLY completing your profile – not just jobs and education; 3. Including appropriate keywords for your industry and areas of interest; 4. Extending your network with both quality AND quantity globally.

Just like a resume, if you do not impress the reader in the first 7-10 seconds, you lose. Though you can change some of your settings, typically the first thing seen in a profile is your photo, name, title, location, and number of connections (the specific number shows until you reach over 500, then "500+ shows, which should be your eventual goal as it demonstrates your connectedness). You want to get to at least 50 connections reasonably quickly to show that you are engaged with this platform. Something that also catches one's eye is a background image. Complete your details in all the fields mentioned above! The steps suggested here are general recommendations. There are exceptions to every rule, but overall, to maximize your effectiveness, you should seriously consider following the steps provided.

6 GETTING FOUND – BOOSTING YOUR PROFILE

Now to boost your profile so that you get FOUND:
19. Your picture is worth more than a thousand words. Ideally. you want to be smiling, making eye contact, with just you in the picture. A Harley t-shirt might be appropriate if you are working for Harley or projecting a biker image, though even in that case I would still think twice. Project your most positive image. You also need to consider the background having it match the nature of image you want to project. You do not want to take shortcuts here. Your image should compliment your brand. Are you a professional, capable, friendly person radiating confidence, or are you informal, sloppy, and not real serious about how you present yourself. You decide. Go to the *Me Tab*, click on *View Profile*, click on your picture in the upper left. Then *add* or *change* your photo – there are also some basic cropping and rotation options built-in, along with limited editing capabilities for filtering, brightness, and contrast. Click *Save Photo* to continue.
20. Photo tips for consideration. Besides eye contact with the lens and a smile, you want to make sure your photo looks and feels professional. You also want to make sure there is good lighting. A headshot that is not too close and not too far away is desirable – a full head and shoulders shot. Consider the law of thirds (do some digging to

understand the concept) in your photo's composition. Teeth should be showing, but there should not be a large gap between your top and bottom teeth. Raised corners of the mouth are also suggested in conjunction with your smile. Consider the color warmth of your photo (color balance) and brightness as well. Be sensitive to having proper contrast in your photo too.

21. To analyze your photo, try using tools like www.Snappr.co (Australia) and www.Photofeeler.com (Colorado, U.S.) for a free analysis of your LinkedIn and other social media photos.

22. Your Background Photo (Banner) is separate from your headshot photo. It can be changed by clicking in the background area *on the screen* next to your photo or clicking on the *little pencil* if there is one. Find something inspirational, ideally related to your professional interests or reason for being on LinkedIn, consistent with the brand you are seeking to build to display. Crop, filter, and other adjustments, similar to when you added your individual picture, are available. You can even create your own image with a quote using a tool such as Canva at www.canva.com for free. Searching for images in Google can also be effective but be careful of copyright considerations. *Apply* when done.

23. Now to edit your name, headline (your headline should highlight your greatest strength/s or what you are trying to let people know are your unique

talent/s), and current position. Select the option as to whether or not to *show your education* (encouraged) in the intro. Choose other options if desired. Click the little *pencil icon* next to the Add profile section and the More... button. You can optionally enter a former/maiden name. This is also where you choose your country, location (which shows on the first screen of your profile), postal code, and industry. You can also drill down to enter personal access contact information such as phone, URL, address, and birthday (no year). Hints: For your name, keep it simple. If you want to add titles and certifications you can but be careful not to overpower. Some folks say to be different by using all caps for your name or inserting a symbol or two to set you apart. Others say be like everybody else for consistency in appearance. This is really up to you. My personal preference is to show a little flash but be professional and keep in mind why you are here on LinkedIn. Your headline needs to be MORE than just a job title or "want work" (or other words to that effect). If you are on LinkedIn, you are likely open to people finding you and conversations about opportunities. What are you especially good at or proud of? What is your personal tag line? What is the message you want to communicate to people that look at your profile? Make sure to *Save* when you have completed your edits.

7 ENHANCING YOUR PROFILE

Now it is time to Add/Edit profile sections to round out your listing. Go to the areas by clicking on *Add Profile Sections*. This is where you use keywords, but not cliché words, to set you apart. You are telling a story to sell yourself, make it an interesting one:

24. When selecting *Intro*, you can also change your photo here (if you had not already done so). Indicate the type of job interviews you are pursuing if you are seeking such opportunities. Job titles and locations are the two criteria you can include. Note, you can limit your eligibility indications to recruiters only or open it up to all members on LinkedIn.
25. Summary is the first section you can edit under *About*. You can add a paragraph or two introducing your capabilities. Don't hold back – if you can't brag about yourself who can? You do not want to exaggerate or sound arrogant. It's a balance, like anything else. So why would someone want to reach out to you – here is where you tell them! In this section, you also want to emphasize keywords that are recognized in your industry and areas of interest that you want to be associated with as would be used by others. LinkedIn searches will take keywords from virtually all areas of your profile, especially your introduction, jobs, and education. So where can

you find keywords? Get the job descriptions of positions that you might want to aspire to from job sites and use THOSE words. This is what employers will be searching for. You need to make your summary SHINE. And needless to say, no typos or grammar challenges please. You can grammar tools like grammarly.com to perform a spelling/grammar check. But be warned, such tools are NOT infallible. ALWAYS Proofread, then Proofread, and Proofread again. Then have somebody else Proofread your profile. There are some powerful built-in tools that will let you print out your profile to review directly in a resume format. You should definitely take advantage of them. We will be discussing those later.

26. Next on the Add Profiles section is the *Featured* area. This is the place that shows things you added including posts of your own content or shared articles you have initiated in LinkedIn. The next category, *Add a Link* allows you to specifically add your videos, articles, presentations, and other outside content. Sharing your knowledge and giving exposure to its members is at the core of LinkedIn's purpose. By sharing and helping others it reflects back on you, like a mirror. It also earns you credibility in your field. Note, for uploaded documents, there is a limit of 100MB, a maximum of 300 pages, no more than one million words, and the only accepted file formats are .pdf, .ppt/x, .doc/x, and jpg/ jpeg, Media such as photos, documents, and presentations can also be added.

27. Now to share background information talking about who you are. This includes Job/s, school/s (grades and dates optional), Licenses, Certifications, and Volunteer experience helping you to tell YOUR story! Keep in mind the keywords and accomplishments that you want to highlight. Here is where you add work experience including dates of employment (optional, though I did find having the dates handy for my own referencing), a headline title/role, and a description, You have the option to upload media, presentations, photos, and documents associated with your employment here, and are encouraged to do so. You can also turn off the "share with network" flag that announces new positions and schooling. You probably want to turn this off while initially making multiple changes to your profile so that your network is not inundated with your new jobs and other changes. On the other hand, if you are taking on a new role, it is nice to have LinkedIn automatically communicate that to your network on their *Notifications* tab. You can also add the same information and media links to your school activities and descriptions...and you want to!

28. *Skills* is the next category. You want to include specific skills and talents that relate to your field and interests – you can add up to 50! These are also things that your network can and will endorse YOU on confirming their knowledge of your experience in these areas. Think what knowledge

you possess that differentiates you from others. What programming languages or other software skills do you bring to the table? What other capabilities do you have to offer? This also goes along with keeping keywords in mind that someone who might want to find you might use to search to reach out to you or someone with a similar background having similar skills. Make sure to hit *Add* when done.

29. Accomplishments are things you want to showcase. The specific proposed categories in LinkedIn include: Publications, patents, courses taken (including MOOCs – free courses further discussed later), projects, honors & awards, test scores, languages, and community organizations. Be creative and be complete! As an example, I added to my language listing "Accounting," which although I teach currently in the university setting, I firmly believe it is the language of business. Colleagues have specifically commented to me after seeing that. Find things EVERYWHERE that will set you apart!

30. Under *Additional Information*, you can request recommendations from your connections. It will then ask you for your professional relationship as well as your position that they would have known you from. Listed are positions/job titles you previously entered with your job's information. It will also help you immensely if you take the initiative and give reference letters for your contacts and not just ask for references from

others. BOTH, given and received references are published in your profile and adds strength to your profile. It sends out a signal that you are a giver and not just a taker. It can sometimes help to draft a sample reference letter that you can give to a person writing about you which gives them additional ideas that they can put in their own words. Make it easy for people to give you references!

31. The *Adding Profiles in Another Language* option helps showcase you to a broader audience. Make sure you are fluent in the language that you indicate so that when they respond to you, normally in their native tongue, you want to be able to respond in kind. There are 23 supported languages and 22 unsupported as well as the proverbial "other."

32. Earn displayable badges from taking courses or other online seminars (https://www.mooc-list.com/ and www.mooc.org are good sources to investigate such classes, usually free or at a low cost – even classes from Wharton, Stanford, IBM, Harvard, and MIT are available). If you are a LinkedIn premium member, you have free access to thousands of courses at LinkedIn Learning that you would want to highlight as part of your profile.

33. Take LinkedIn's Skill Quizzes for free. They are found through *the Skills & Endorsements* section where you can earn badges by taking quizzes and showing your proficiency in software usage. Included is the full Microsoft Office Suite (Word,

Excel, etc.), Google Analytics, a variety of programming languages, and even QuickBooks and WordPress. Quizzes are in English only, take 15ish minutes to complete, and if you are in the 70th percentile or above, you earn a badge for display in your profile. These are likely to be skills that you already included in your skills and endorsements section. They even have a couple of practice example questions if you want to experience what the questions are like. Upon passing, you can optionally display your badge though you are encouraged to do so!

34. Monitor your *Profile Strength*, which in edit mode, is indicated above the *About* section. You want to be recognized as an All-Star by LinkedIn for maximum exposure. Note: You are already an All-Star by my definition for committing to taking the initiative and building your brand using this powerful tool. Congratulations!

35. Make sure to complete ALL sections in LinkedIn to maximize your exposure and search-ability based on the information you present. This also gives you the most opportunity to include keywords that gets you found!

36. As a status check, go to the *Me tab*, next to the Add Profile Section, and click on the *More* Button. Select *Build a Resume*. Now print it out and review. You may also choose *Save to pdf*, which is right above the Build a Resume choice. It will download a pdf to your browser. It offers a little nicer formatting than your LinkedIn straight

resume. For many, It is can be easier to read your information from a printout for editing purposes than editing on screen. You can also directly insert this content into grammar and spell checkers as previously discussed.

8 SECURITY AND PRIVACY CONSIDERATIONS

Now that you have set up your profile, enhance your ability to be found in searches, and included things that will get you notices. Let's talk security and privacy settings. You have many potential options to review. A couple of suggested highlights are included below. Under *Me*, where you went to edit your profile, the next category is Settings & Privacy. Let's go to this area.

37. Under the *Account Tab in Settings and Privacy* you can edit your email addresses, phone numbers, passwords, and a variety of other preference settings.
38. Under *Privacy* you see sections relating to: 1. How others see your profile (this includes search engines and other resources outside LinkedIn as well as categories they can see). Note: You can also *Create a Badge* here with your LinkedIn link that can be inserted into blogs, websites, or other outside media; 2. How others see your activity; 3. How LinkedIn uses your data; 4. Your Job Seeking Preferences; and 5. Blocking and Hiding. You probably want to scan all the settings but make sure to specifically look at 1. and determine what you want the public to see vs. what you want your 1st degree connections to see.

39. * Make sure under category 1. above, in the Public Profile Settings, that you *edit your URL*. LinkedIn starts with a URL address of: www.linkedin.com/in/fname-lname-###X###XX. You can EASILY edit that so it turns into a vanity URL, something like www.LinkedIn.com/in/DrScottCPA so that when you include this link in signature blocks, resumes, and on presentations, it looks A LOT more PROFESSIONAL. You can also reach this customization by clicking on the *Edit Public Profile and URL* from your *Me* page found next to your background photo. You are also welcome to connect with me at the second link above, further expanding your network and adding over 16,000 2nd degree connections!

40. Also in category 1, you want to specify who can see your connections, either *you* or *you and all your connections*. Keep in mind that for competitive reasons, you may want to limit such access. On the other hand, you may feel that being open is a plus to those that connect to you. It is also a great source of potential connections that your 1st degree connections with access for you to be able to see their connections. You can also disable display of your last name to 2nd and 3rd degree connections. 1st degree connections can always see your last name (though even if disabled, folks searching for you can enter your last name and find you).

41. From option 2, you can *enable/disable* the flag that allows other users to know if you are on LinkedIn or not (active status) as well as whether you leave a trail when viewing other profiles (they can see you peeked). The default trail shows your name and information. You can change the flag here if you would rather be more anonymous and have the other person see "Someone on LinkedIn" rather than your name. Normally I want to let people know that I was interested in them for one reason or another, but sometimes you may not want competitors to know you were checking on them. Other strategic considerations might have you not wanting to leave evidence of your visit.
42. From option 3, you can *enable/disable* Share Job Changes, Education Changes, and Work Anniversaries from Your Profile. You decide if you want to have these things communicated to your 1st degree connections. You normally would want to keep this active, which is the default, so that your network knows when changes occur. You might want to disable temporarily when making major updates to your profile to prevent an onslaught of notification emails reaching your contacts.
43. Option 4 is where you can indicate whether you are open to recruiter searches when they have opportunities.
44. Option 5, among other things, allows you to block users and removes you from their "Who's Viewed Your Profile" section so they don't see that you

were there. As described above, a trail is left when you look at someone's profile.
45. Under the *Ads* tab you have choices in choosing to make the LinkedIn ads targeting you more relevant. They can and will target ads to you based on your attributes and those of your 1st degree connections (defaults to yes).
46. Under the 4th and final Settings and Privacy tab, *Communications*, you can set whether you welcome all invitations, or want to be invited only by those folks that know your email (the former is recommended and is the default as it adds an extra layer of challenge for someone trying to connect with you). You can also set the flags, normally enabled, whereby LinkedIn sends you email notifications when you get messages or invitations to connect. Those notifications can be turned off here.

9 SEARCHES & EXPANDING YOUR NETWORK

Let's talk Searches, located on the upper left corner of the page. This is where you can do your own research, find friends and colleagues, see company pages which includes a listing of most of their employees on LinkedIn, find personal and professional groups of interest, explore alumni from schools you have attended or plan to attend while being able to reach out directly to contact them for help and insight.

47. Growing your network is as easy as typing in a name in the search field, hitting enter, and locating the appropriate listing. Often, especially with popular names, if you don't see the name right away, you will need to refine your search.

48. You can refine your search using the bar that starts People, Jobs, Content, More. A little further to the right you see three filters: *Connections* (as in degree, 1st, 2nd or $3^{rd}+$), *Locations* (you have to pick a larger city near where your contacts might be), or *Current Companies*. If you hit the *All Filters* button to the far right, you get additional demographic options such as schools, industries, past companies, and more. Sometimes in your search, even though you typed in a first and last name, it shows other names similar or related, so you may need to go into *All Filters* and specify that first and last name in the appropriate field.

49. When you find a person that you would like to connect with, click on their *name* and go to their

profile. Then find the displayed *Connect* button (if they are not 2nd degree connections, you will have to go to the *More...* button on their profile and then select *Connect*). When you choose *Connect*, MAKE SURE TO CLICK ON *ADD A NOTE* rather than Send Now. You want to personalize every invite so that you maximize your chances for getting accepted and connected. If you invite too many folks to connect that don't remember you, or you just feel that they would be a good contact and they really don't know you, you are setting yourself to not only be rejected by that person, but also to be placed on restriction by LinkedIn. If you get too many rejections, LinkedIn will restrict your invitation requests so that with every request you will need to type in each person's individual email address – a major inconvenience as you may not know it! The number used to be five rejections (over a specific time). I am not sure if that limit has changed or not. Believe me, I know the frustration of having to type in addresses each time! Early in my LinkedIn experience, I was guilty of tagging and requesting connections to lots of professionals that I wanted to get to know. When they indicated that they did not know me, LinkedIn flagged my account requiring typing of the email address EACH time I made a request. If this happens, you can communicate with LinkedIn support directly for help and they will normally, as a courtesy, remove that flag if you are nice about it...once. Which brings me to another point. In your Summary area, you want to include contact information such as your email address, and possibly other ways to get a hold of you. This will help if someone really wants to find you and they either require this email address to connect, or they want to reach out to you directly outside of LinkedIn.

50. So what about companies? Well, if you type in a Company name (sometimes you might need to choose the *More* button next to People, Jobs, and Content and choose *Company*) you can go to a Company Page. From an organization's Company Page, you can follow (encouraged if you have an interest in being alerted to articles and news items about them), or learn more about their company – almost like a web page. Especially handy is being able to click on *see all X,XXX employees on LinkedIn*. If you have any connections working there you will see a link that you can click on to see them. Additionally, if you click on the link to all employees, you have the same screening tools and filters as you used to search for people in the previous bullet point and be able to choose titles and location (for multi-location organizations), along with schools. This feature is very handy when searching for allies at a company.

51. And now for the power of Groups! You can join up to 100 groups related to personal or professional interests. But why would you do that! First and foremost, you get to network and know fellow professionals that either you can help down

the road or that can ultimately help you. Useful articles and information is posted here. Questions of mutual interest are answered regarding things YOU and THEY are interested in! If and when you post regularly you become recognized as an authority and the go-to person relating to a particular topic. It also happens to be a back door to sending messages, as you can normally only send messages within LinkedIn (InMail) to first degree connections on your free account. Paid accounts usually have a limit of 15-20 InMails a month to non-1st degree connections. But in groups you can send free messages to your non-1st degree connections. You can even start your own groups related to your interests. Groups can have two members, hundreds of members, hundreds of thousands of members, or over a million members. Think of the exposure opportunities! Groups can be publicly listed or private. Groups can be open where everyone is welcome. Some require the approval of the Group's Admin/s to be admitted. People that see your profile can also see what groups you belong to and who you are following (though that can be disabled individually by group if you choose). As a matter of fact, when you look at someone else's profile, check out the groups they belong to. If you find something interesting just click on that group and you will be transported there and be able to make a request to join. Normally to find a group of interest, type a topic in the search bar, click on *more*, and select *groups* (although sometimes a group will pop up without having to select the groups category). As an example, if you typed in Finance and, selected groups, the first listing (Finance Club) is a group with over 1,000,000 members. The second, third, fourth, and fifth each have over 200,000 members. There happens to be 100 pages (screens) for Finance with about 10 on each page for this category. You may want to play with refining your search terms if you discover a large number of groups.

52. The power of Schools is similar to that of groups. Go ahead and try typing the name of a school you either graduated from or would want to potentially go to. Select *Schools* from *More* if you need to. From the school's page, you will have access to the Number of Alumni on LinkedIn, your connections currently working there on LinkedIn, if any, and most of their employees that are on LinkedIn. You will also have access to lots of information along the left margin including: About, Jobs, Alumni, Videos, and more. To see the real power, NOW SELECT *ALUMNI*. Click *on Show More*. You will now be able to see Where They Work and the number of alums with each of those organizations. If you click on one of the companies, you will now see below the Names, Titles/Positions, and Shared Connections that you might have with these people, in addition, you can click on them and directly access their profile. Talk about a lead list to gain insight about a

company you might want to work for or sell to! This can even be used if you are interested in exploring career insights with someone knowledgeable. What would you do if a student from your alma mater called you and said (or you were the student making that call) "Hi, my name is X, and I am currently a student at your alma mater, Y University. I noticed you are working at a company in the exact job I think I might like to pursue when I graduate – though not taking yours of course! Would you have some time to talk with me, obviously at your convenience, so I can understand how to best prepare for such a role?" Would you say no? Might you even invite them to meet for lunch and a company tour? Most folks who get that call would love to help. I would…and I have! Even if a company you might be interested in is not listed in the top 15 that are displayed, you can type in a company name in the search, right under where it says number of alumni, to see if any alumni might have been at or are employed by that organizations. Try entering in FBI in the search box – I found 5 current employees from one of my schools, with 10 others that were previous employees. And ALL of them show up by name and picture (if they originally included one) below. You are just a click away from accessing their profile. You also can see in other columns where alumni live (and click on those particular bars if you want to just see people in a certain area). You can further see what they studied and what they do by clicking *next* and seeing the next two columns. Finally, by clicking *next* again, you see what they are skilled at and if you have any 2nd degree connections that might be able to introduce you to people at these organizations. You might even find 3rd degree connections that you can reach out to.

53. Forensic Linking – yes, I made that term up – I will suggest a process to seek out people in case you need to do some digging to find their LinkedIn profile. Make sure you type the name correctly in the search box as LinkedIn is very syntax sensitive. If you transpose (reverse) two of the letters in their first or last name, you will usually not see the person you seek in the list. LinkedIn is pretty good with shortened first names like Pat vs Patricia (though not so good with Jay vs Jason). If you enter Pam and the individual use Pamela, or vice versa, it is likely they will still be listed. If the person includes a title like Dr. in front of their name, they will also often not appear near the top of your search, if at all. Sometimes, when you type a name, you will see hundreds or thousands of names listed. You have the option of looking at each name (good luck with that) or you might try to revise your search using filters as previously mentioned. Note: not all names match the first and last name you entered, so 20 screens of names may not be as bad as it looks. Often, the LinkedIn algorithm will propose people it thinks you might be interested in finding based on commonalities (such as industry, companies, or geography) or

parties related to those that you are searching for using the name as a starting point. The easiest way to narrow down the list after entering a name in the search box and hitting return is to *enable all filters*. The first filter I would enter is the Last name filter. Make sure to click on *Apply* after each refinement in your search. You also want to change fields one at a time, possibly even removing previously entered criteria. If you enter too many specifics, you might screen out the person you are looking for by being too restrictive. Linked takes an AND approach rather than an OR approach when you apply filters. If this does not give you the desired results, choose your next known (or assumed) fact. You could possibly use the location by city (in the U.S. you need to usually narrow it down to a cities metropolitan area – I wish they did state but no such luck. If outside the U.S., you can type in a country without a specific city being needed), industry/s you think they fit in, schools they may have attended, current companies, or past companies. Again, it is helpful to not be too restrictive and delete one field while substituting another. The premium subscriptions do give you a few more search field options. For each category you will see five options as proposed by LinkedIn based on their algorithm. If none of those are what you are wanting to use, as you start typing, you will see alternatives for which you can check the box to apply that criteria. Outside of LinkedIn you can try to use Google searches to find companies, places, and schools for the person of interest. Also, as mentioned in previous steps, you can use the School or Company areas to find alumni and employees as well. Happy searching!

54. If you are looking to purchase products or services, you can search and seek out people in an industry that are connected to you or to your contacts. Maybe you are looking to set up a merchant account. If you type merchant account and you may want to limit your search to 1st degree connections, you can specify that. You might recall that there is someone in your network in the industry and just do not remember their name or company. You can easily find them searching in this manner. Searching through 2nd degree and other connections gives you added depth with which to find vendors.

55. Which leads us to using Boolean Logic in searches. In short, you can use quotes for exact matches of terms, and AND/OR/NOT (make sure to USE UPPERCASE) to include or exclude members. Parentheses are encouraged for multiple selection criteria. You can also type a list WITHOUT the AND if you type two or more terms. The AND will be assumed.

56. So you may ask "Do I connect with people that I don't know" or "Just people I know and can vouch for?" Well that depends on your motivation for being on LinkedIn. But frankly, if expanding your network and connecting with people is the purpose of being on LinkedIn, as it is for many of us, why

wouldn't you connect? Let's talk about how LinkedIn prioritizes searching through one's connections. The way LinkedIn's search algorithms function is that if you are looking for someone having certain search terms in their profiles LinkedIn will usually check a person's 1st degree connections first, then continues to reach out to 2nd degree connections, and then finally outside to other connections. So what is a 1st degree or 2nd degree connection? All people you are connected to that have accepted your invite, or those you have accepted theirs, are 1st degree connections. Once you are connected, ALL of their connections become YOUR 2nd degree connections. Starting to see the potential? All of my connections are 2nd degree connections (unless they are already 1st) to everyone else in my network. This means that if one of my 16,000+ connections searches for specific terms on the search bar, if I meet the criteria, I will be high on their list. But if one of my 1st degree connections meets their criteria, now a 2nd degree connection to the original searcher (through me), they will rise in the search list too. Therefore, USUALLY, the more connections the merrier, as it gives you and your connections better access to showing up in search results. That being said, you may want to connect only to persons with whom you might have common interests or goals. Or you might also want to consider yourself being an Open Networker (or LION – LinkedIn Open Networker) where you are willing to connect to any legitimate member that asks. That is your choice. As an example, I travel a lot, am prior military, have owned and worked for a number of businesses, served on several boards, received degrees from three AACSB business schools, taught at multiple universities, and have connections from a variety of countries with a variety of interests and skills. If I am invited to connect I will typically say yes fairly quickly - especially with HR, C-Suite, Entrepreneurs, and Academics, as I feel they could all ultimately benefit my students and other 1st degree contacts. But as soon as I accept and within hours receive the "I have a business opportunity for you", click, I will usually *Remove Connection* (under *More* on their profile screen). Again, the decision is up to you and depends on the motivation of why you are here in the first place.

57. So how else do I expand my network? From your main LinkedIn page, next to the Home button, select *My Network*. In the center, there are often suggested Companies or Individuals to follow, Hashtags to add, suggested Groups to join, or recommended People to add to your network. You can click on them to join or connect. One downside of this method is that you are NOT able to personalize your message, so I usually would discourage this technique unless you are pretty sure they remember and know you. As an alternative, you can click on their name, go directly to their profile, and then click *Connect* (if

2nd degree) or Go to *More*, then choose *Connect* (if 3rd degree or more).
58. There is also a *Grow your Network* button to the left on the same *My Network* tab. You can either blast all your email contacts at once, which I again discourage, or if you cannot locate a particular individual through normal searching methods, you can click on the *Grow your Network* link in the left margin, and next to the Outlook and AOL buttons, go to the *email icon/picture*. Clicking on that allows you to insert one or multiple email addresses (multiples need to be separated by commas and NOT a ";" like Outlook, unfortunately) and send an email invite directly to these individual/s. If they currently do not have an account, they will be invited to set one up. Spread the word and the wealth!
59. So what does the *Home* tab offer? It is usually where you first land when entering LinkedIn. It lists articles and postings of interest that may be linked to your Interests (Influencers, Companies, Groups, and Schools) and is also where YOU may *Start a Post* about something that you find interesting and want to share. You want to check this area frequently, maybe even daily! Not only will you read interesting posts by others in your network but you will also have the opportunity to post items that you find interesting and that you think might benefit others. Anything of interest, including pictures and links, may be posted here AND COMMENTED ON– and these posts will

usually go out to your 1st degree connections. LinkedIn might even promote them giving you additional recognition. Note: You can do the same in the Groups you belong to sharing for all Group members to see. You can even make a comment and insert a URL link to an article. This means that you don't have to write an article to be able to share it.

60. The *Jobs* tab allows you to search for jobs and internships. LinkedIn will also post suggestions that it thinks might fit your interests. This is also where you can post a job if you are looking for employees or help.

61. The *Messaging* tab is where you receive InMails (and some advertising by folks sending out InMails) from your 1st degree connections and sometimes premium (paying) members and advertisers. You can reply very easily as well as add links and files. InMails have a reputation of getting more attention than traditional emails outside of LinkedIn. Additionally, unless disabled, your connections will receive an email that they have a message on LinkedIn. Messages are also stored here and are searchable almost indefinitely.

62. Let's export a backup copy! LinkedIn acknowledges that the data is YOURS (though they also have full access, hmmm). Now that you have worked so hard to build your profile and network you want to make sure that you have a backup copy of your contacts and other information. Click on *the My Network* tab, then

click on the *number* where it shows you your number of connections. On the next screen, towards the top right corner, at the same level of where you find ### Connections, click on *Manage Synced and Imported Contacts*. On the far right you will see an option to *Export contacts* (this may also be found under settings and privacy, in the How LinkedIn uses your data section, *Get a Copy of Your Data*). You will then go to a screen that allows you to select either *Download* the larger data archive, or just specific pieces of information. I suggest you do the *Download larger data archive* as you will get multiple files. You will receive an email when the report is completed. You will then be able to download a .zip (compressed) file that when you click on it will automatically open into a number of CSV file (comma delimited file, which means you can directly open it in Excel or another spreadsheet). If you just check just connections, you will just get the first name, last name, company, position, and date connected. If you want to get email addresses for your contacts (at least the email they had shared initially with LinkedIn) you would also need the Contacts file from the larger data archive.

63. The second to last item I will mention directly regarding what you can access from your profile is the *Notifications* tab. Here you will receive notice of promotions, graduations, job changes, the "Daily Rundown" (daily news article summary) as well as birthday notification of your 1st degree

contacts. You can message them directly from this area.

64. Finally, I will let you know where to find Help with any and all of these features, besides using a Google search which is also a good option. From the *Me* tab, click *Help*. If you need to reach out to a live person, click on *Ask the Help Community* and scroll to the bottom where it says *Contact us* (it is well hidden as I suspect they prefer that you use the automated answers, which are usually pretty good too). If you choose not to scroll all the way down for personal attention, you can *Search Discussions* in the forum. Your first line of help is clicking on *Help* from the *Me* tab, and then typing into the Search box what you are seeking help with. It will suggest links to solve your issues, again, usually very helpful.

10 LINKEDIN STRATEGIES

A. Fundamentals of Strategy in Using LinkedIn: Suggestions to Maximize YOUR Return on the Investment of your time and energy.

65. If you think that just by setting up a great account, connecting to a bunch of people, and now you can just sit back and now enjoy the benefits of your efforts, you are WRONG. Like any garden, you reap what you sow. Your LinkedIn presence requires continuous nurturing to be effective. How serious are you about having LinkedIn work for you? When you answer that question and commit to maintaining continuous and consistent effort, you will be able to enjoy the benefits beyond your wildest expectations. Does that mean you have to spend an hour a day to maintain your LinkedIn presence? Probably not, though some people do a lot more (especially initially). You should commit to spending an average of at least 15 minutes a day to explore, reach out, connect, and help others in order to start to really see a return on your investment of time in LinkedIn. But you WILL see a return and amazing benefits from your commitment! Just like a web site, your profile and engagement needs to be consistent and updated regularly to stay fresh. Adding postings of new articles, videos, papers, presentations will help build your presence and credibility. This is THE place to strut your stuff. You just got an award?

Post it! You attended a conference and picked up some useful information? Share it! You presented at that same conference? Share a link to your presentation and let people know about it.

66. Remember to STAY POSITIVE (also known as no negativity, but that sounds a bit negative). By being positive and upbeat, your connections will respond in kind. If you permeate negativity, then that is what will be reflected back at you. My mama taught me that if you can't say something nice, don't say it at all. In the military and in management (for the most part) I learned a useful management lesson: commend in public and criticize in private. LinkedIn is a public forum. Before hitting that post button, even though you do have editing capability after the fact, reread your post – multiple times if possible. Bad spelling or grammar can also be very embarrassing.

67. There are givers and there are takers. On LinkedIn, you need to be both! Givers provide value to their network such as information and access to contacts and resources that help them succeed in their efforts. Only giving will most likely burn you out. Being just a taker is probably worse (ok it _is_ worse) in that eventually your network will get tired of you taking and not giving back and will then stop helping you. Most of us have a natural tendency to want to help one another, especially our friends, colleagues, and family (although I guess it does depend on the family too). But it is also ok to ask for favors and

help. As a matter of fact, when you give there is often a psychological commitment by the receiver to want to give back. There is nothing wrong with asking for help which also helps cement a relationship. It is a two-way street, as is life!

68. Don't forget to personalize invitations to connect. Help the prospective connection to remember you by reminding them of how they know you and what the benefit is TO THEM by connecting with you is (yes, the WIIFM, What's In It For Me, from the other person's viewpoint). Keep in mind you normally have a limit of 300 characters in an invitation which goes very quickly when initiating an invite. Always be prompt (don't wait a month or even a week after you meet someone) when sending invitations and be polite. Make it about them with a closing such "I would be honored to be added to your LinkedIn professional network."

69. Don't be afraid to take the initiative and reach out to someone that you may not have yet met but know that you will be meeting them in the near future. This means that when going on an interview or appointment, there is nothing wrong with asking your (already connected) contact "So who else will I/we be speaking with?" You may then reach out to those "strangers" with words to the effect "X, I am excited to meet you next Tuesday when I interview for the XYZ position! I would also be honored to be added to your LinkedIn Professional Network!! In appreciation of your consideration, Y." Though some might

interpret this as overly aggressive, most (including myself) feel that getting the extra exposure to your name will give you an edge and added recognition as they hopefully (don't worry, they will) remember your taking the initiative. The reward is likely greater than the risk, but such an initiative might not impress everybody. On the other hand, do you want to work in an organization that penalizes you for taking extra initiatives? As you know in marketing it usually takes multiple exposures before successfully closing of a sale or getting the job offer. This is one more exposure.

70. You know a resume needs a balance of content and white space. It also needs to be PERFECT grammatically and have zero spelling errors. Formatting also needs to be consistent. Your profile is a public statement of your attention to detail. I would hate to tell you how many candidates I have rejected after reading a well-organized and presented resume, whereupon checking their LinkedIn profile, there were so many grammar and spelling errors, or inconsistent capitalizations (even one error is too many), that they were rejected just based on my LinkedIn inspection. Frankly, I would look at a person's LinkedIn profile before my resume review. The consistency of LinkedIn's format helped me focus on areas that I thought important. And yes, as discussed earlier, the 7-10 seconds you get when someone reviews a resume carries over to LinkedIn, unless something piques the

interviewer's curiosity and they dive a little deeper. I have interviewed hundreds of candidates along with thousands of resumes and LinkedIn profiles. You get to the point that you are sometimes looking for any excuse to reject a candidate. So don't give them one!

71. So let's talk buzzwords…AVOID THEM! The same way you want to stay away from buzzwords on your resume you want to eliminate them in your LinkedIn profile as well. Also, consistent with your resume, you want your profile to document successes. Be sure to quantify the results associated with your accomplishments. Tell YOUR story in an engaging way that draws the reader in. Make your profile a welcoming environment filled with positive energy. Keep in mind that you typically also want to talk in the first person (I did this) rather than in the third person (this was accomplished). Include multimedia and links everywhere you can, as long as it doesn't redirect your reader to a competitor or to an outside site that they may not return from. Check your links periodically to make sure they still work!

72. Speaking of resumes, as mentioned previously but it bears repeating, don't forget to include your LinkedIn vanity URL in the address block of your resume with your physical address, email address, and phone number. It demonstrates that you are connected to a professional social network and smart enough to change it to a readable form. Also

include your URL in the letterhead of your stationary, in the signature block of your emails, and on all presentations that you make. You can even use your LinkedIn URL when another software package or social network asks for your web site. Your URL IS your website.
73. Visual content IS powerful, and it is the wave of the future. You can record your own videos very easily in Zoom or create your own YouTube channel for free. Things you create, including videos, belong in LinkedIn!
74. Use LinkedIn tools for creating content and authoring. There is a publishing platform that is built into LinkedIn. It helps you increase your visibility with LinkedIn's search algorithms moving you up in LinkedIn searches. At the top of the Home page where you would normally enter a post at *Start a Post*, immediately underneath, you will see the link to *Write an Article in LinkedIn*. Do so! Add headlines, images, and a compelling story. Enhance your exposure and increase your opportunity to be recognized.
75. Stalking or Creeping may sound like something you shouldn't normally do (and The Police's song Every Breath You Take or Blondie's One Way or Another are a little creepy, well okay, a lot creepy when you listen to the words), but in LinkedIn you can go in stealth mode, as described previously, to hide your visits to another person's profile.
76. Speaking of creeping, there is another powerful backdoor to making connections, as well as seeing

who might be scoping you out. Under notifications you will periodically be notified that "XX YY and ## others **viewed your profile**." You are then able to click on *See all views* and find out who some of them are. Not only does this show you names (usually) of people checking you out (premium versions so all views, unpaid only some), it also lets you know if they are a 1st, 2nd or 3rd degree connection. This additionally gives you insight into who is looking at your profile AND is a prime opportunity to invite 2nd and 3rd degree potential additions to your network, giving them the opportunity to connect with you. Clicking on their picture or name will take you to their profile where you can then customize a connection invite. They were obviously looking at you for a reason. Why not give them another opportunity to see that they were right in seeking you out in the first place.

77. One item to monitor when looking at your profile, or that of someone else's, is the *People Also Viewed* area. This shows you what other folks people that are looking at you are also finding during their search. It works the same as you look at your contacts profile so you can see who they are attracting. Maybe there is someone you know or want to know. This is powerful for seeing what your perception is within the LinkedIn universe as well as telling you if your competitors are also being considered.

78. When asked to rate someone's skills on LinkedIn, if you can, do so! It is also valuable for you to

receive skills endorsements. Make sure the skills you are being endorsed for are the ones you want. You can reorder or remove the ones you might prefer to be deemphasized or eliminated.

79. Monitor the reactions and endorsements to your postings. These are often the kind of folks that appreciate what you do and would be worthwhile to invite to be a personal or professional connection. React positively and insightfully to postings by others. They WILL remember you and hopefully be open to connecting with you or even reach out to you when they have a question or need.

80. Get the LinkedIn Mobile app. More than half of LinkedIn users access LinkedIn through this app. You can also send voice messages 20-60 seconds long (only in the app) from your phone by hitting the microphone when you are preparing your message. This does NOT work from the desktop version, although the desktop version overall has a lot more functionality and messages can include images, attachments, and emojis. Also, if you request to connect from the mobile app, the generic invite will be automatically sent. To customize from your phone or tablet, tap the "..." button on the contact's profile page. You also want to periodically look at your own profile to make sure that it is mobile-friendly, presenting your mobile presence in the best light.

81. Connect! Connect! Connect! Give! Give! Take! Share! And COMMIT to making your LinkedIn

efforts strong and consistent. It will pay off! MAKE time to create the best profile, provide the best feedback, create the best articles, and include the best images and videos. Be all you can be (ok stole that one from the Army, even though I was Navy, but for adults, I guess it is considered sharing not cheating or stealing). Log in AT LEAST 3-4 times a week and keep things fresh!

82. LinkedIn is one more tool in your toolbox, albeit a very powerful one. Reach out to your connections in real life to build rapport, relationships, and friends. People do prefer to buy from, employ, and support their friends.

83. A cool mobile feature if you are ever presenting and want to promote LinkedIn connectivity between participants is available to connect folks in close proximity through their mobile phones or tablets. It is called the *Find Nearby* feature. This allows people in the same room to connect very easily (with you and with others). To initiate do the following: Have participants take out their cell phones; Make sure Bluetooth is turned on; Go to the *mobile app* (which over 50% of LinkedIn users are currently using anyways, even more than the desktop version though I personally prefer LinkedIn on the desktop most of the time); Tap *My Network*; Find the *Add Contact Icon* (a picture of Head and Shoulders with a "+" sign); Click on *Find Nearby*. You will then see others close by that have initiated the same process and can directly connect with them. There is also the

potential of scanning a QR code instead of Find Nearby if you are in a one-on-one (or two) situation.
84. This is a networking tool. So go network! Help others and you will be helped. Inspire others and you will be inspired. Make others rich and they will make you rich (and that is not just about the money!).
85. Share YOUR LinkedIn passion with others. It WILL come back to you with many thanks for inspiring their participation.

11 Afterword

I hope you found the above information useful and will be able to apply it to your needs! I also would be honored to be added to YOUR LinkedIn professional network (and if you don't ask, you don't get)! Please feel free to reach out with any questions, comments, or connection requests to me at:
http://www.LinkedIn.com/in/DrScottCPA

Wishing you continued success,

Dr. Scott

ABOUT THE AUTHOR

Scott Dell, CPA, MBA, MAE, DBA

Dr. Scott is an experienced accountant (CPA), educator (UW-DBA, Wharton MBA), entrepreneur (multiple industries), manager, learner, salesperson, technologist, Navy veteran, and business professional. He has experience owning, operating, and growing businesses. He thrives on helping others to grow their organizations, expand their knowledge, and educate their people while using the latest technologies. He even used to sell vacuum cleaners door-to-door and pre-owned (okay, used) and new cars.

His passion for business and education has led him to inspiring others as a full-time educator entering academia as a university Accounting Program Director for 13 years in Wisconsin. He has relocated to South Carolina and continues to teach and learn. Areas of expertise include accounting, business, nonprofits, Model UN, and technology, as well as conducting classes teaching others to learn to ride motorcycles safely (MSF Certified) and photography. He also shares his extensive LinkedIn knowledge liberally. His service to others through board of director efforts is another way Scott gives back.

Dr. Scott brings a level of understanding that helps him inspire others. Scott shares his business acumen, communication skills, and enthusiasm with passion. Having 20+ years of business experience, international business, and personal travel/global awareness, along with 10+ years of full-time academic teaching and program management, Scott combines the best of academia with direct application to business practices.! Connect with Scott at http://www.LinkedIn.com/in/DrScottCPA or email Scott.Dell@FMarion.edu.

www.ingramcontent.com/pod-product-compliance
Lightning Source LLC
Chambersburg PA
CBHW071122240526
45465CB00022B/779